COMMUNITY · CONNECTIONS

?

WHAT DO THEY DO?
VETERINARIANS

BY JOSH GREGORY

CHERRY LAKE
Publishing

Published in the United States of America by Cherry Lake Publishing
Ann Arbor, Michigan
www.cherrylakepublishing.com

Content Adviser: Paul DeMars, DVM, DABVP K9/Fe, Oklahoma State University, Center for Veterinary Health Sciences, Community Practice
Reading Adviser: Cecilia Minden-Cupp, PhD, Literacy Consultant

Photo Credits: Cover, pages 1 and 17 ©iStockphoto.com/monkeybusinessimages; page 5, ©Felix Mizioznikov, used under license from Shutterstock, Inc.; page 7, ©Mark William Penny, used under license from Shutterstock, Inc.; page 9, ©iStockphoto.com/MarkHatfield; page 11, ©iStockphoto.com/izusek; page 13, ©blickwinkel/Alamy; page 15, ©iStockphoto.com/CREATISTA; page 19, ©iStockphoto.com/stevecoleccs; page 21, ©iStockphoto.com/Darkcloud

LIBRARY OF CONGRESS CATALOGING-IN-PUBLICATION DATA
Gregory, Josh.
  What do they do? Veterinarians / by Josh Gregory.
    p. cm.—(Community connections)
  Includes bibliographical references and index.
  ISBN-13: 978-1-60279-810-6 (lib. bdg.)
  ISBN-10: 1-60279-810-9 (lib. bdg.)
  1. Veterinarians—Juvenile literature. 2. Veterinary medicine—Juvenile literature.
I. Title. II. Title: Veterinarians.
  SF756.G744 2010
  636.089/069—dc22   2009042806

Cherry Lake Publishing would like to acknowledge the work of The Partnership for 21st Century Skills. Please visit www.21stcenturyskills.org for more information.

Printed in the United States of America
Corporate Graphics Inc.
July 2010
CLFA07

VETERINARIANS

CONTENTS

WHAT DO THEY DO?

A DOCTOR FOR ANIMALS

You notice that your dog is sleeping a lot. He usually plays and runs around all day long. "I don't think he is feeling well," you tell your mom. Mom bends down to pet him. "I think you're right," she says. "Let's take him to see the veterinarian."

Your pet is important. If he is sick, he needs to see a veterinarian.

Veterinarians are doctors who treat only animals. They are also called "vets." It takes years of hard work to become a vet. Vets study why animals get sick. They also learn how to treat different animals. They learn to care for tiny birds and big elephants.

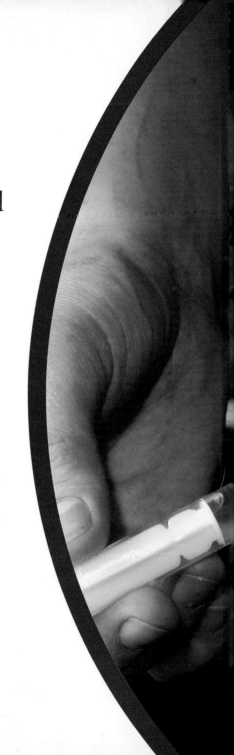

Vets treat big and small animals.

LOOK!

Take a look around
next time you are at
the vet's office. How
is the office like your
doctor's office? How
is it different?

7

Vets have a love for animals.
Treating animals takes patience.
Animals may not understand that
the vet is trying to help them. They
might try to bite or run away.

Vets also need to be good
with pet owners. They try to
answer the owners' questions.

Vets have to work well with both pets and owners.

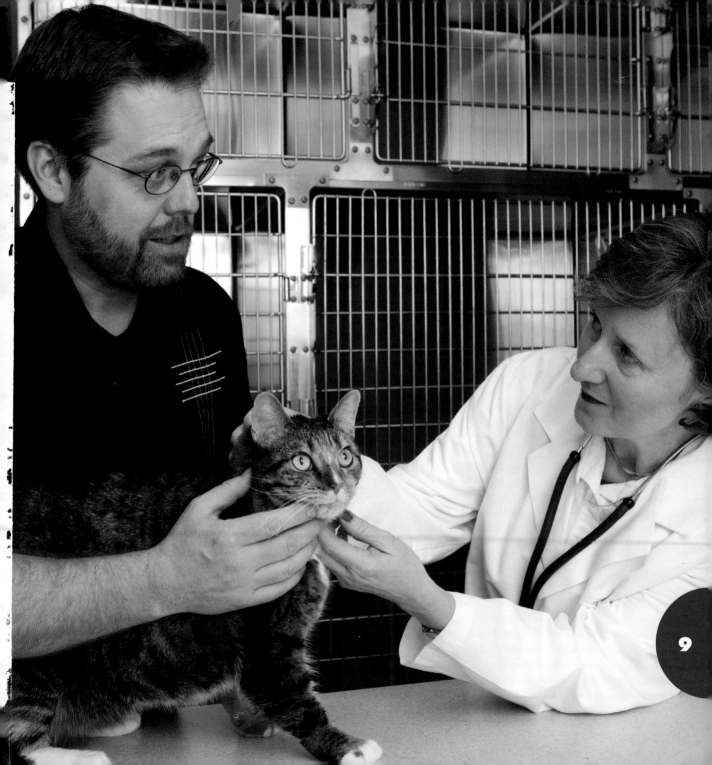

A VET'S DAY

Vets spend most of their time doing checkups. Animals cannot tell us when they are sick or hurt. Vets **examine** animals to see if anything is wrong with them. They listen to animals' hearts and lungs. They talk to pet owners about keeping animals healthy and safe. They also give advice about good pet food.

Vets give animals checkups to keep them healthy.

Animals with fur need protection from fleas and ticks. These bugs can spread illnesses.

Many animals also have to be protected from worms. Worms can get inside animals and make them very sick.

Vets give animals **medicines** to keep these creepy crawlers away. Vets also give animals **vaccines** to prevent **rabies** and other illnesses.

Animals get vaccines to prevent illnesses.

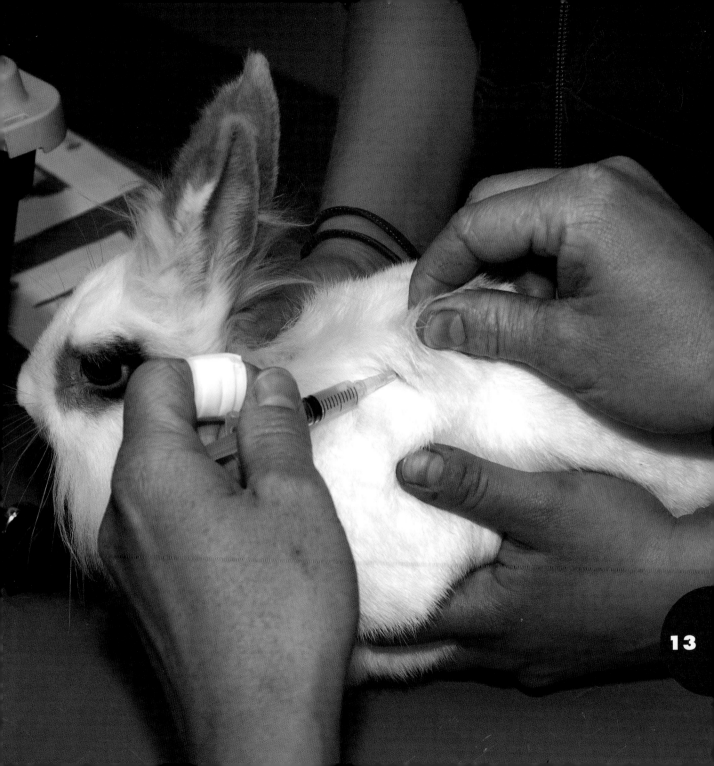

13

Animals can get hurt just like people do. Vets use **X-rays** to check for broken bones. They put on casts. They also stitch up cuts.

Vets perform **operations** on some animals. Often, vets need to work at night or on weekends. Animals could need a vet at any time!

Vets sometimes perform operations on pets.

One operation is performed to keep an animal from having babies. Most dog and cat owners have this done on their pets. Why do you think this is important?

DIFFERENT VETS FOR DIFFERENT ANIMALS

Most vets work only with pets. They might see dogs, cats, or birds. Some people have uncommon pets. These might be lizards or ferrets. Their owners have to find special vets to treat their animals. Other vets work on farms. They might treat cows or horses.

Some vets treat horses and other farm animals.

Ask your pet's vet what animals he or she works with most. What is the strangest animal he or she has treated? You might be surprised at the answer!

17

There are also special vets who work at zoos. They might treat giraffes or monkeys. They could also treat dolphins or eagles. What other animals are found in zoos?

Other vets study illnesses. They do **research**. This helps them discover new ways to help animals.

Some vets try to make new medicines for animals.

Your dog is feeling a lot better since his trip to the doctor. The vet gave him some medicine. Now your dog is running around just like he always does!

Vets work hard to keep our pets healthy. Remember to thank your vet the next time he helps your pet.

Thank your vet for all his hard work!

GLOSSARY

examine (eg-ZAM-uhn) to look at very closely

medicines (MED-uh-suhnz) drugs used to treat a sickness

operations (op-uh-RAY-shuhnz) procedures in which bodies are cut open to repair damaged parts or remove diseased parts

rabies (RAY-beez) a dangerous disease that is spread by the bite of an infected animal

research (REE-surch) a study or investigation of a certain subject

vaccines (vak-SEENZ) shots that help prevent diseases

X-rays (EKS-rays) special pictures that show parts of the body that cannot be seen from the outside

FIND OUT MORE

BOOKS

Ames, Michelle. *Veterinarians in Our Community*. New York: PowerKids Press, 2010.

Hutchings, Amy. *What Happens at a Vet's Office?* Pleasantville, NY: Weekly Reader, 2009.

WEB SITES

FutureVet
www.futurevet.net/
Learn what you need to do if you want to become a veterinarian.

The University of Georgia College of Veterinary Medicine: Animal Doc
www.vet.uga.edu/VPP/animaldoc/index.php
See how vets operate on different kinds of animals and read some facts about animals.

INDEX

24

ABOUT THE AUTHOR

Josh Gregory writes and edits books for children. He lives in Chicago, Illinois. Veterinarians have been a big help to him when his dogs have eaten things that they shouldn't.